"Home is Where the Heart Is:"

"Home is Where the Heart Is:"

A Family History of the
Descendants of Daniel and Emma Monk

Daniel and Emma

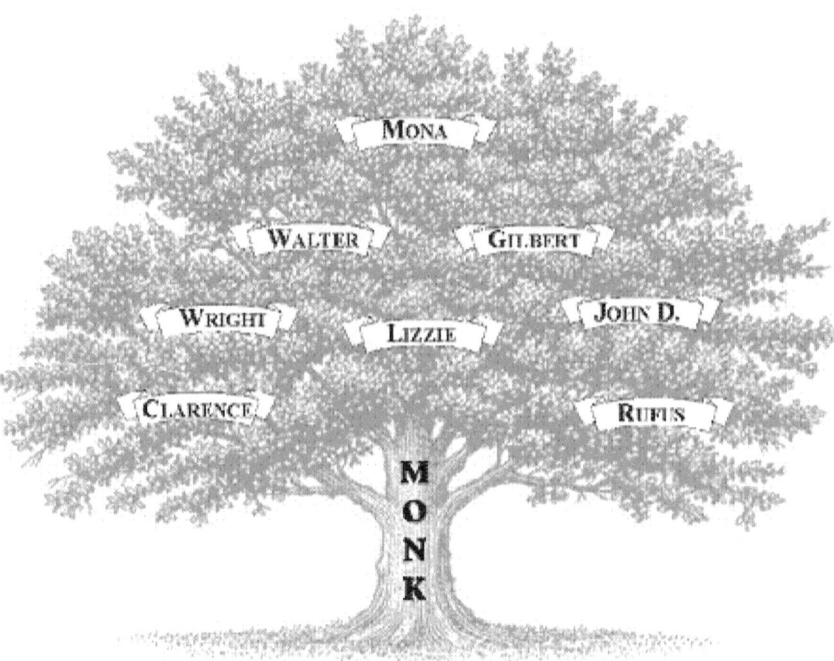

MONA

WALTER GILBERT

WRIGHT LIZZIE JOHN D.

CLARENCE RUFUS

M
O
N
K

Ricardo Morgan, MA

To order additional copies of this book, contact:
Xlibris Corporation
1-888-795-4274
www.Xlibris.com
Orders@Xlibris.com
78707

Contents

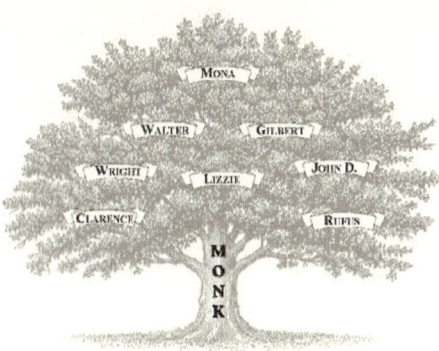

Introduction

It is with much pride and great anticipation that we present the history and family lineage of the Monk family of Onslow County, North Carolina. Our family heritage is rich with great stories of perseverance, triumph over adversity and joy through the tears.

The Monk family presents this volume as a token to our future generations. It is a token of life, love and living for the Master. It is a token of aspiration, inspiration and elevation. This is the legacy for our future generations to learn and to educate themselves about who they are and from whence they came.

This family is a people that loves God. This family is a people who understand their very roots. We understand the sacrifice and the trails that were blazed for those of us younger Monks. We will NEVER forget! We will NEVER minimize the sacrifices, the trials, and the tribulations that were done on our behalf.

This volume is dedicated to all of those ancestors, starting with Daniel and Emma Monk. If it were not for the love they shared with each other, we wouldn't be here today. And to all of those descendants of Daniel and Emma that sacrificed, blazed the trails and were willing to even put their lives on the line so that we today, would have the hope for a better life.

It is our prayer that as you read through each of our family members that you will find a greater appreciation for not only our family but your individual family and the rich history and the story within the family.

Ricardo Morgan, MA
Monk Family President and
Scholarship Chairman

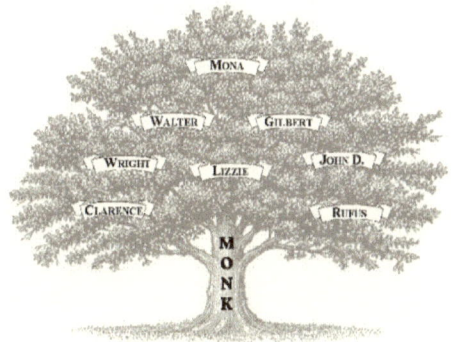

Acknowledgments

There are countless people to whom the Monk family is indebted for making this project come to fruition. This project has been in the talks for years, literally, without ever getting any traction. It was out of planning for the 30th Monk Family Reunion in 2010 that the family decided that we would put our talk to action.

We first give all glory and honor to God for allowing us to do this project. Without Him, nothing would be possible. We have to also thank the Monk Reunion committee that spent countless hours in not only preparing our great family reunions for the past 30+ years, but they spent a great deal of time in planning this publication. Special recognition goes to Patricia Brannon, Veronica Davis, Corinthia Lopes, LaShanna Spicer, John L. and Sonja Monk. Two very special workers on this project: Frank Lopes, who is also the Monk family webmaster and Valerie Williams, who is our publicity coordinator and was responsible for editing and providing quite a bit of valuable feedback and insight. A special thank you goes out to each and every family member and consultant that participated by giving us personal information, interviews, photos, and other jewels to make this volume a success.

Lastly, to the family members that submitted photos, biographical information and articles, every effort was made to include as many of them as possible. Due to the age, size and condition, some photos and content were not able to be edited with high enough quality to be included in this volume but we did seek to include as much information, history and accuracy on each side of the family tree as possible.

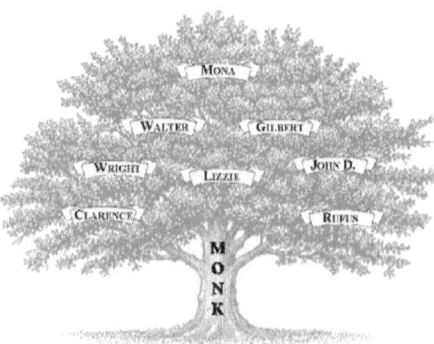

Special Family Dedication

The Monk Family owes quite a debt to the matriarchs of the Monk Family who were the driving force behind putting this volume together, Nancy Isabel Monk Murrill and Geneva Monk Pickett. Mother Nancy is currently the oldest living descendant of Daniel and Emma Monk and Mother Geneva is the youngest living descendant. These two virtuous women have exemplified the characteristics of Godliness. They opened their homes, shared precious family relics and gave countless hours to do interviews, and shared valuable historical information.

The wise King Solomon had it right, when he describes the attributes of a virtuous woman in Proverbs 31:25 and following. He said, "Strength and honor are her clothing; and she shall rejoice in time to come. She opened her mouth in wisdom and in her tongue is the law of kindness . . . . Favour is deceitful and beauty is vain; but a woman that feareth the Lord, she shall be praised."

Mother Nancy and Mother Geneva are perfect examples of these attributes. They have been the backbone for many in our family for a number of years through joyous times and through sadness and tragedy. We look to them for guidance, nurture, support and love. The Monk Family is pleased to dedicate this volume to these two virtuous women.

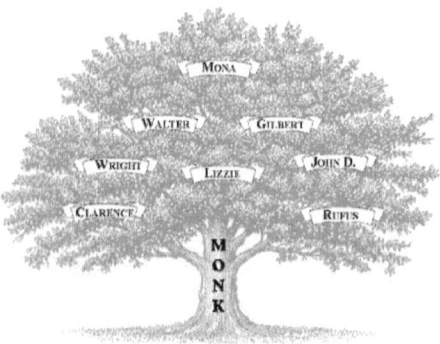

The Monk Family History: "The Love Story"

It has been said that some time during the 19th Century, a handsome young gentleman by the name of Daniel Monk met a beautiful young lady, Emma Shepard. There is not a lot of information known about the two other than Daniel had three half-brothers: John Monk, David Ward and Alonzo Ward. Mother Emma was originally from the area now known as Maple Hill, North Carolina. Soon after their acquaintance, their friendship blossomed into a beautiful relationship and the two were united in holy matrimony. To this great union was born eight children, two daughters: Mona and Lizzie and six sons: John, Gilbert, Rufus, Wright, Walter and Clarence. Mona was the first of the children to pass away as she died as a young child and Rufus was the last child to pass away during the 1990s.

All total, there were 45 grandchildren and countless great grandchildren and other descendants. As of 2010, there were six living grandchildren of Daniel and Emma Monk: **Nancy Isabel Monk Pollock Murrill**, daughter of John Daniel and Rena Monk is the oldest living grandchild, **Ollie Bryant Monk**, youngest son of John Daniel, **Alnita Monk Rollinson**, youngest daughter of Clarence and Mary Monk, **George Monk and Geneva Monk Pickett**, all children of Wright and Annie Monk and **Lucenia Dixon Hardison**, daughter of Lizzie Monk and Isaac Dixon. Geneva is the youngest of the six living grandchildren. Sadly, **Vernon Monk**, son of Wright and Annie Monk was among the living descendants until January 23, 2010.

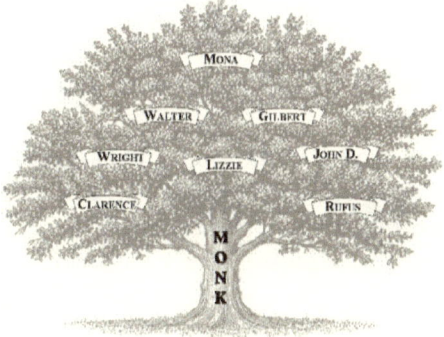

John Daniel Monk

(1883-1971)

John Daniel Monk was the oldest son of Daniel and Emma Monk. His name came from his father's brother's first names, John and Daniel. He was born in Verona, North Carolina on April 30, 1883. At an early age, he ventured out and started working for the railroad company in Wilmington, North Carolina. He moved there and worked for years until the job transferred him to Jacksonville Atlantic Coast Line Station. He married Rena Bessie Murrill, his childhood sweetheart in 1910 and unto this union 9 children were born: James Edward, Joseph Daniel, Catherine Lee, Nancy Isabel, John Moses, Judge Robert, Mary Elizabeth and twins Ollie and Olive.

John worked for the railroad station for over 40 years and he also had a family farm which his wife, Rena basically ran while he was working. He was also a member of the Mason and Elks Society until his death in 1971 at the age of 88. He is buried in the Monk Family Cemetery on Country Club Road.

John Daniel's Family Tree
John and Rena Monk

James *	*Joseph* *	*Catherine* *	*Nancy*	*John* *	*Judge*	*Mary*	*Ollie*	*Olive* *
		Raymond	Annie (Tot)*	Junetta	Clementine*	Lillie	Vicki	Henrietta (Pumpkin)
		Nehru	Della	Doris	Joyce*	Kenny		Daphne
		Rena *	Hannah	Robert	Judge Jr.	Pat		Ronald (Boo)
		John	Juanita	Dexter	Garnette	Benjamin Jr.		
		Clara Ruth	James *	Tracy				
		Veronica	Louise	Malcolm				

*Deceased

James Edward Monk

James Edward was born on September 11, 1911 to John Daniel and Rena Monk. He was the oldest child born to this union but died as an infant in 1912. There are no known photos of James Edward and he is buried in Murrill Hill Cemetery. His gravestone is in the shape of a diamond.

Joseph Daniel Monk

Joseph Daniel was born on March 9, 1913 to John Daniel and Rena Monk in Verona, North Carolina. John was a proud U.S. Navy veteran and served in World War II. He met and married Alma and was married to her until her passing. He was the second oldest of the Monk children. Joseph lived in Norfolk, Virginia once he left Onslow County for the military. He passed away in March 1996.

Catherine Lee Monk Morgan

Catherine Lee Monk Morgan was the third child and first daughter born to John Daniel and Rena B. Monk on August 25, 1915 in Verona,

North Carolina. Catherine (Cathy Lee) married Willie Raymond Morgan in 1947 and unto that union six children were born: Raymond, Nehru, Rena, John, Clara Ruth, and Veronica (Dee-Dee). Catherine worked in Custodial and at Furniture Fair for a number of years. She was a faithful member of the Bell Fork Church of Christ until her passing on September 30, 1992. Today, her tree includes 13 grandchildren, 18 great grandchildren and 3 great-great grandchildren.

Catherine Monk Morgan in her younger days

Catherine's Tree

Raymond was born in 1949 to Catherine Monk and Willie Raymond Morgan. He is the oldest of Catherine's children and currently resides in Daytona Beach, Florida. He is married to Florene Morgan and has been married for over 30 years.

Nehru was born in 1950 and served his country in the United States Army for 22 years. He married his sweetheart, Ute, and was married to her for over 30 years before her passing in 2008. He is the father of three and grandfather of five and great grandfather of three. He currently resides in Tacoma, Washington where he works as a trainer and supervisor for Olive Garden Restaurant.

Nehru's Tree

Johnnie Mae is the oldest child to the union of Nehru and Ute. She is the mother to Damita, George and Ashley.

Damita is the oldest daughter of Johnnie Mae but was primarily raised by Nehru and Ute. She graduated from high school and served in the military and is the mother to three children.

Dale is the only son of Nehru and Ute. He is the father of two, a daughter and a son. He is currently in Minnesota.

Rena is the oldest daughter of the late Catherine Lee and Willie Raymond Morgan. She was born on January 30, 1951 and graduated from Jacksonville High School. She worked in cosmetology and is the mother of two, Delphine and Ricardo. Rena passed away on October 6, 2003.

Rena's Tree

Delphine Morgan was born on March 20, 1972 in Jacksonville, NC to Rena Morgan. She is the oldest child of Rena. She graduated from Jacksonville High School and currently works in the medical field in Charlotte, North Carolina.

Ricardo was born on July 6, 1979 in Jacksonville, NC to Rena Morgan and William Hunter. He graduated from Jacksonville High School and East Carolina University. He received his Masters degree in technical professional communication in 2005. He worked as an educator in the public schools all the way to adult education. He is currently CEO and Founder of RLM Development Solutions which is a business consulting company. His company has worked with various organizations, for profit and non profit organizations such as HIV/AIDS centers, churches, restaurants and senior citizen homes.

John Daniel Morgan was the baby son of Catherine and Willie Raymond. He was born in 1952. John worked in construction for a number of years and was a dedicated member of the Bell Fork Church of Christ. He currently resides in Tacoma, Washington with his brother Nehru.

Clara Ruth Morgan Heyward was born to Catherine on April 1, 1954. She did a number of jobs throughout her life. She was married to Harold Heyward for a number of years. "Ruth" is the mother of five: LaShanna, Cecil Jr., Felicia, Harold Timothy (deceased) and Hakeem. She is also the grandmother of seven grandchildren.

Clara's Tree

LaShanna was born in 1974 and graduated from Jacksonville High School. She met and married Kendall Spicer in 2004. She currently works on Camp Lejeune and is the mother of three daughters: Stephanie, Symone, and Daysha.

LaShanna's Daughters

Cecil was born in 1976 and currently works in the hotel industry. He is the father of four children: Khalil, Arinna, Alillia and Alina.

Felicia was born in 1985 to Clara and Harold Heyward. She graduated from Swansboro High School and East Carolina University. She currently works and lives in Greenville, North Carolina.

Harold Timothy Heyward was born in 1988. He was a football standout and was actively recruited by a number of colleges and universities. Tragically, he was killed in a car accident just weeks before he was set to graduate from Swansboro High School in 2007.

Harold Timothy "Tim" Heyward (1988-2007)

Hakeem was born in 1991. He is the youngest child of Clara and Harold Heyward. He is currently a senior in high school at Swansboro High School and resides in Hubert, North Carolina.

Veronica Denise Morgan Noland Davis was born in 1956 and is the youngest child of Catherine and Willie Morgan. She met and married Jesse Noland and moved to Alabama for 19 years before returning to Jacksonville and marrying Donnell Davis. She went to Beauty school in Columbus, Mississippi and has been a seamstress for 33 years. She currently works aboard Camp Johnson as a seamstress and is the mother of three sons: Antonio, Adrian and Justin and she is grandmother to seven.

Veronica's Tree

Antonio was born in 1974 to Veronica and Jessie Noland. Antonio graduated from high school and matriculated to the University of Alabama. He also served in the United States Marine Corps Reserves for twelve years. He is currently an educator in Winston-Salem, North Carolina and is married to the former Kimberly George and is the father of six children: Antonio Jr, Aaron, Ashley, Justin, Alexis and Toni.

Adrian was born in 1976 and is currently living in Alabama. He served in the United States Army for four years and he is the father of one daughter, Adrieanna.

Justin was born in 1980 and graduated from Jacksonville High School. He currently lives in Jacksonville with his mother.

Nancy Isabel Monk Pollock Murrill

Nancy Isabel was born on November 24, 1917 to John and Rena Monk. She was raised primarily by her grandparents. She met and married Walter Pollock until his demise. She later met and married, Daniel Murrill and was married to him until his passing in 1985. Nancy is the mother of six: Annie (Tot), Della, Hannah, Judy Juanita, James (Buddy) and Louise, grandmother of nine, 17 great grandchildren, and 3 great grandchildren. Nancy is today the oldest living direct descendant of Daniel and Emma Monk. She is the oldest descendant on both her father's side and her mother's side.

Nancy's Tree

Annie Beatrice "Tot" Pollock Tate was born in 1938 to Nancy Monk and the late Walter Pollock. "Tot" moved to Phoenix, Arizona at the urging of her aunt Olive Shepard and lived out there for the rest of her life. She helped rear three cousins as her own: Henrietta, Daphne and Ronald Shepard. Tot died in November 1987.

Della Louise Pollock Nuell was born in 1939 to Nancy Monk and the late Walter Pollock. Della worked at Onslow Memorial Hospital for several years before moving to New York where she lived for a number of years before returning to Jacksonville. She is the mother to four: Dion, Wanda, Pernell and Lamont and is the grandmother of nine.

Della's Tree

Dion Pollock is Della's oldest child. He currently resides in Laurel, Maryland with his wife Judy and daughter Leslie. Dion is the proud and healthy recipient of a liver transplant back in 2005 and is doing well today.

Wanda Pollock Jackson is the only daughter of Della Pollock Nuell. She was in the military, but now works as an EMT. She is married to Victor Jackson, a sergeant major in the United States Army. She is the mother to two sons: Kevin, who is married and is in the military stationed in Georgia and Victor Jr (VJ) who is in college at North Carolina A and T University.

Pernell currently lives in Jacksonville and is a military veteran. He is the father of three sons and one daughter.

Lamont is the youngest son of Della. He graduated from Jacksonville High School and is currently in the U.S. military and is stationed in Hawaii. He is married to Marisa "Missy" Pollock and is the father of two: Dana "Dee Dee", currently in college, and Lamont Jr (LJ).

Hannah Pollock Maxwell Wright is the third daughter of Nancy Murrill. Hannah lived right next door to her mother for a number of years. She was married to the late Sam Maxwell for a number of years. She is currently married to Romeo Wright and lives in Fayetteville, North Carolina. She is the mother of three children: Greg, Thomas and Thomasena and is grandmother to six.

Hannah's Tree

Greg is the oldest child of Hannah's. He served the country in the U.S. military for a number of years and recently retired from the military. He currently lives in Germany with his wife and has two daughters: Samantha, currently in college and Joelle.

Thomas is the second child of Hannah. He currently lives in Fayetteville, North Carolina. He is the father of two children: Phillip, currently in school and Adrienne. Adrienne was a rising senior at

Fayetteville State University when she was killed in a car accident in January 2008.

Adrienne Dineen Maxwell

Thomasena is the only daughter of Hannah. She is a licensed pharmacist in Jacksonville, North Carolina and is the mother of two children. LeAndra, a senior in high school and Malcolm, also in high school.

Judy "Juanita" Murrill Robinson is the daughter of Nancy and Daniel Murrill. She married Milton Robinson and moved to Brooklyn, New York where she currently lives. She has one daughter, Tonita and two grandsons.

Judy's Tree

Tonita is the only daughter of Judy and Milton Robinson. She currently lives in Brooklyn, New York where she works with Special Needs children. She is also the mother of two sons.

James Edward "Buddy" Murrill is the only son of Nancy and Daniel Murrill. He was born December 21, 1948 in Jacksonville, North Carolina. Buddy was a graduate of Jacksonville Senior High School and furthered his education at North Carolina A and T University in Greensboro, NC. He served his country in the U.S. Air Force and worked at the Piccadilly restaurant chain for a number of years. He is the father of one son, Jason. Buddy Murrill passed away on July 18, 1988 after an extended illness.

James Tree

Jason is the only child of James Murrill. He is a college graduate and currently works in the medical field in Charlotte, North Carolina where he lives.

Louise Augusta "Lu Lu" Murrill Graves is the youngest child born to Nancy Murrill. She graduated from Jacksonville High School and North Carolina A and T University. She currently lives in Laurel, Maryland where she works for the FDIC.

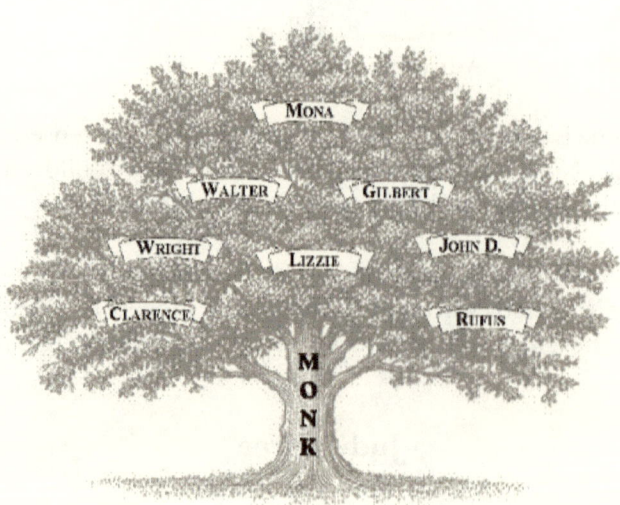

John Moses Monk

John Moses was the fifth child and third son born on January 24, 1920 to John Daniel and Rena Monk in Verona, North Carolina. Dad was born and raised in Onslow County where he continued to live as a young man. During the years of his youth, America was immersed in Jim Crow, but never was it able to steal dad's smile. He met and married Gladys Eucile Chapman on September 7, 1941 and was married to her for over 40 years until her passing in 1984. To that union, seven children were born: Junetta, Doris Elaine, Robert Stanley, Kenneth O'Dell (Deceased), Dexter Ray, Tracy Erwin, and Malcolm Ross.

At the onslaught of World War II, he wanted to serve his country so he volunteered for the United States Army. During the war, he spent time in several places in the country, the Pacific area and even across the world. At the end of his enlistment, he decided to take advantage of the GI Bill and he went to school to become a brick mason. During his early days, it was not always easy to find employment and was forced to leave town many times. He went to places such as Pittsburgh, Pennsylvania, Baltimore, Maryland, and Norfolk, Virginia, before finally landing employment on Camp Lejeune. John also worked in the educational system teaching masonry at White Oak High School and at Coastal Carolina Community College. He later married Pearl Owens. He was a faithful member of the Bell Fork Church of Christ until his death on March 14, 1999. Today, his tree includes at least 11 grandchildren and 14 great grandchildren. There are so many accolades that could be paid to him but I think to let it be known how we, his family, remember is important.

Gladys and John

He was as:

A SON	exemplary	**A BROTHER**	enjoyable
A FRIEND	dependable	**A HUSBAND**	reliable
A PERSON	stupendous	**A FATHER**	responsible

And most of all, he is missed!

(Submitted by Doris Monk-Smith)

John's Tree

Junetta Brown Sharpless is the oldest child of John and Gladys Monk. She graduated from Georgetown High School in 1959 and has retired from two major companies and currently lives in Garner, North Carolina and is married to James Sharpless. She is the mother of two sons: Wayne and William "Billy" Brown. She is also the grandmother of two: Jonathon and Jasmine and is expecting a great grandchild this year.

Doris and Emmette Smith

Doris Elaine, the second daughter of John and Gladys Monk was born on January 31, 1944 in Anniston, Alabama. She married Earl Dorsey Freeman in 1961 and had two children, Kent Kozart and Cheryl LaVaun. After a subsequent divorce, Doris married Emmette Randolph Smith and to that union one son, Okesa Sean was born. Doris has five grandchildren: From Kent there are four grandsons, Arnold Sheppard, Destin Keyvond, Arie G'Kente and Kent Kozart, Jr. Cheryl LaVaun has one daughter, BreAnna Alexiceya LaVaun Vidot. After spending thirty-two years in the state of New York working in corporate America, she moved to Virginia in 1993, and started a new profession, teaching Virginia's secondary students. She is currently retired and still resides in Virginia.

Robert and Wilma Monk

Robert Stanley Monk was born in Jacksonville, North Carolina on January 25 to John and Gladys Monk. He grew up farming on the family farm on Country Club Road. He attended Georgetown High School, where he met Wilma Brown. He and Wilma married after high school while he was stationed at the United States Air Force base in Warner Robbins, Georgia. According to Robert, "our oldest son, Stanley was born on Warner Robbins Air Force Base and once his four years in the Air Force ended, he went to school on the GI Bill to learn air conditioning, refrigeration and heating. After he finished school, his first job was with Humphrey Heating and Cooling where he installed heat pumps. Robert and his family later moved to Wilmington, NC to work for another company for a year before he was hired to work in civil service at the New River Marine Corps Air Station. Robert passed the North Carolina Contractor's Exam in 1975 and was licensed for the state of North Carolina. He retired from the Camp Lejeune School System as supervisor for the maintenance department for 15 years. He along, with his wife Wilma, who retired from Sprint Telephone Company in New Bern, NC, are currently enjoying retirement by playing golf up to 5 times a week. Robert started coaching football when his son Stanley was 10 and coached both Stanley and his youngest son, Quincy. He coached for a number of schools here in Onslow County in both Football and Basketball and while he coached White Oak High School's basketball team, their team was number one in the state for two years in a row and went three years undefeated.

Robert's Family Tree

Stanley Monk, the oldest son of Robert and Wilma Monk, was coached by his father and eventually the hard work paid off because he received a full football scholarship at Duke University in 1984 and he graduated in 1988. He even had NFL ambitions and worked out with the Dallas Cowboys but an injury ended his football career. Stanley is married to his wife, Chareen, and they are the parents of four children, Trey, Jordan, Myles and Jacob and they currently live in Clayton, North Carolina.

Quincy Monk, the youngest son of Robert and Wilma Monk was born on January 30, 1979. He also was coached by his father and his hard work paid off too because after graduating from White Oak High School, he received a full football scholarship the University of North Carolina at Chapel Hill in 1997. After graduating from college in 2001, he also had NFL ambitions and was drafted by the New York Giants. Quincy is married to his wife, Lisa and just became the proud parents of Naomi Aria Monk this month. They currently live in the Raleigh, North Carolina area.

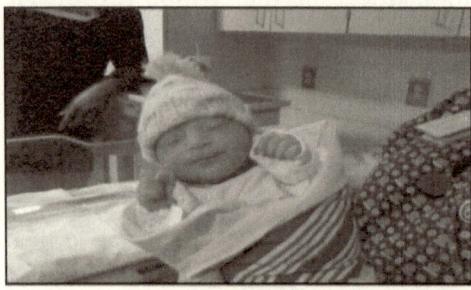

Naomi Aria Monk, Daughter of Quincy and Lisa Monk

Dexter Monk is the fourth child of John and Gladys Monk. Dexter was a highly intelligent student and excelled in academics. He was educated at Howard University and Shaw University. During his career, he was a Senior System Engineer at Brocade, a principal, SAN Solution Services, and a Technical Team Leader—Blade Infrastructure Solution Center at IBM. He recently retired from IBM and currently lives in the Cary, North Carolina area with his wife Queen.

Tracy Monk is the fourth son of John and Gladys Monk. He was born on December 18, 1952. Tracy learned the brick masonry trade from his father and continues that occupation today. He also served in the U.S. Army and is a Vietnam Veteran and is the father of one daughter, Tracey Eucile.

Malcolm "Mac" Monk is the youngest child of John and Gladys Monk. He currently lives in Clayton, NC with his wife Cecelia. He is the father of three daughters: Keshia, Precious and Stormie. He is also grandfather of two.

Malcolm's Tree

Keshia is the oldest daughter of Malcolm and Cecelia. She is the mother of two children and lives in Greensboro as a respiratory therapist.

Precious is the second child born to Malcolm and Cecelia. She is currently serving in the United States Air Force stationed in Goldsboro as a meteorologist.

Stormie is the youngest child born to Malcolm and Cecelia. She lives at home with her parents and she is planning on going to college after graduating from high school.

Judge Robert Monk

Judge Robert was born on August 24, 1922 to John Daniel and Rena Monk in Verona, North Carolina. Judge was a proud veteran and served in World War II. He met and married the love of his life, Thelma Pearson and to that union, four children were born: Clementine (Deceased), Joyce (Deceased), Judge Jr. and Garnette. Judge was very active in the local community until his death on December 19, 1964. He was the first person buried in what is today known as Monk Family Cemetery on Country Club Road in Jacksonville. It was said of him at his funeral, "that if Judge Monk didn't make it into heaven, no one would!" That's the kind of life that he lived. Today, his family tree includes at 4 grandchildren.

Judge's Tree

Clementine "Sis" Monk Cospy is the oldest daughter of Judge and Thelma Monk. She was born on May 4, 1943. She married Henry Cospy and moved to California. She is the mother of Erika Cospy and Erika lives in Texas today. Clementine stayed in California until her death in November, 15, 1988, only 10 months after her sister, Joyce.

Joyce Monk was born on October 13, 1944 to Judge and Thelma Monk. She was a beautician and was the mother of one son, Christopher Jones. Joyce died of breast cancer on Jan 3, 1988 and is buried beside her father in Monk Cemetery.

Judge Jr. is the only son born to Judge and Thelma Monk. He was born on Sept 1, 1947. He currently lives in the Baltimore, Maryland area. He is the father of two daughters: Katrina, who currently lives in Baltimore and Angela Chadwick who currently lives in San Diego.

Garnette is the youngest child of Judge and Thelma Monk. She was born on November 18, 1950. She also currently lives in the Baltimore, Maryland area.

Mary Elizabeth Monk Dixon

Mary Elizabeth was born on December 10, 1925 to John and Rena Monk. She met and married James Brannon on December 7, 1941. She later met and married Benjamin Beamon Dixon in 1956 until his passing in 1980. Mary worked aboard Camp LeJeune until her retirement. She was a member of the Bell Fork Church of Christ until her passing in February 2004. She was the mother of four: Lillie, Kenny, Patricia and Benjamin Jr, grandmother of twelve, 7 great grandchildren, and 9 great grandchildren.

Mary's Tree

Lillie Mae Monk Humphrey is the oldest descendant of Mary Dixon. She currently lives in Jacksonville, NC where she retired from work aboard Camp LeJeune. She is the mother of six children, one died as an infant:

Frederick, Sherry, Barbara, Clarence, Maurice and Jackie. She also has seven grandchildren and nine great grandchildren.

Lillie's Tree

Frederick is the oldest child of Lillie Humphrey. He currently lives in Onslow County, North Carolina with his wife Cheryl. He is the father of five children: Tamishka, Lakeila, Frederick Jr, David and Peebles. Frederick also has 8 grandchildren.

Sherry is the oldest daughter of Lillie. She currently lives in Jacksonville with her husband, Terry Cooks. Sherry was a military wife for a number of years now she works aboard Camp Lejeune. She is the mother of one daughter, Shanta, who is an elementary school teacher.

Barbara Jean is the middle child of Lillie. Barbara lives in Jacksonville and worked for a number of years aboard Camp Lejeune until her health caused her to quit. She was the successful recipient of a kidney transplant over eight years ago.

Clarence Ray Jr., was the next son of Lillie Humphrey. He died as an infant.

Maurice is the youngest son of Lillie. Maurice excelled as an athlete during high school. He currently lives in Lithonia, Georgia where he works in the airline industry.

Jackie is the youngest child of Lillie. She also excelled as an athlete even going to the Olympics in Seoul, Korea in 1988. She is the mother of one child, Porsha and she currently lives in Lithonia, Georgia where she works with youth training them as young athletes.

Kenny is the next child in Mary Dixon's tree. He currently lives in Jacksonville with his wife Bernadette and he works in the trucking industry. He is the father of four children: David, Kenya and Kenny Jr. (Boo) and Niki Green.

Kenny's Tree

David is the oldest child of Kenny Dixon. He currently lives in Virginia Beach, Virginia.

Kenya is the daughter of Kenny Dixon. She currently lives in Virginia Beach where she works as a daycare operator. She has one daughter, Kesha'La.

Kenny Jr. (Boo) is the youngest son of Kenny. He currently lives in Jacksonville where he works at Olive Garden.

Nikki is the daughter of Kenny Dixon. She currently lives in Jacksonville and works in a daycare.

Patricia "Pat" is the youngest daughter born to Mary Dixon. She currently lives in Jacksonville where she operates a home day care. Pat is also the secretary-treasurer for the Monk Family Reunion committee. She is the mother of one son, Kevin.

Pat's Tree

Kevin is the son of Patricia Brannon. He graduated from White Oak High School and currently lives in Philadelphia, PA, where he works as a sales representative at Neiman Marcus.

Benjamin "Junior" Dixon is the youngest son of Mary and Beamon Dixon. He graduated from East Carolina University and is currently a franchisee of Chik-Fil-A in Greenville, North Carolina, where he lives with his wife, Tina and two daughters, Cassaundra and Christina.

Ben's Tree

Cassaundra is the oldest daughter of Ben and Tina Dixon. She graduated from South Central High School and is currently attending the University of North Carolina at Greensboro.

Christina is the youngest daughter of Ben and Tina Dixon. She is currently attending school in the Pitt County School System.

Ollie Bryant "Bud" Monk

Ollie "Bud" was born August 31, 1928 to John Daniel and Rena Monk in Verona, North Carolina. Ollie and Olive Monk were twins and were the youngest of the Monk children. Ollie was in the United States Army for over 27 years. He currently lives in Columbus, Georgia along with his wife Martha and he has one daughter: Victoria. He also has 3 grandchildren. He is one of the living original grandchildren of Daniel and Emma Monk.

Ollie's Tree

Victoria is the only child of Ollie Monk. She currently lives in Villa Rica, Georgia with her husband and three children.

Olive Carolyn "Tutter" Monk Shepard

Olive "Tutter" was born on August 31, 1928 to John and Rena Monk. Olive and her brother Ollie were twins and were the youngest of John Daniel Monk's children. She later met and married, Carlton Shepard and to this union three children were born: Henrietta, Daphne and Ronald. She taught Special Education in Roswell, New Mexico for several years. Olive passed away unexpectedly in September 1966 and is buried in the Monk Family Cemetery. Her family today also includes 6 grandchildren and one expected great granddaughter.

Olive's Tree

Henrietta is the oldest child of Carlton and Olive Shepard. She currently lives in Tucson, Arizona where she is retired. She is the mother of two sons, Troy and Dennis.

Daphne is the second daughter of Carlton and Olive. She also lives in Tucson, Arizona along with her husband, Mitchell Langston and three sons, Andre, Mitchell and Matthew.

Daphne's Tree

Andre is the oldest son of Daphne and Mitchell Langston. He currently lives in the Tucson, Arizona area where he works.

Mitchell is the middle son of Daphne and Mitchell Langston. He lives in the Tucson, Arizona area where he works. He is also expecting his first child in April 2010, a baby girl.

Matthew is the youngest son of Daphne and Mitchell Langston. He also lives in the Tucson, Arizona area and works as a barber.

Ronald "Boo" Shepard is the only son and the youngest of the Shepard children. Ronald is serving his country in the U.S. military and currently lives in San Diego, California. He is the father of one son, Ron Jr.

Mona Monk

Mona Monk was the oldest child of Daniel and Emma Monk. Not much is known about her because she died at a very young age. There are no known photos of her since she died as a young child.

Gilbert Monk

Gilbert Monk was the second son and third child of Daniel and Emma Monk. He married Bertha Rhodes and to this union one son, Andor was born.

Gilbert's Family Tree

Gilbert and Bertha Monk

*Andor**

There isn't a lot of information about Andor Monk. However, Nancy Murrill remembers him vaguely growing up. She remembers a time when her mother, Rena Monk was taking care of then, her children, Joseph, Catherine and Nancy as little infants and their cousin Andor during the midst of a terrible storm. Mother Rena was scared of the storm so she set out to go to her parents' home for safety while her husband John was away at work. While she was walking with the children, the wind blew so hard that her hat flew away and she never saw that hat again.

Rufus Monk

Rufus Monk

Rufus Monk was the third son and fourth child of Daniel and Emma Monk. He married Dollie Humphrey and unto this union 10 children were born: Raleigh, George, Nora and Dora (twins), James, Prince Roy, Beulah, Ruth, Nannie and Blanche. He was later married to Sarah Monk. He lived the longest life out of all of Daniel and Emma's children. He was in his mid-90s when he died in the 1990s.

Rufus's Family Tree

Rufus and Dollie Monk

Raleigh*	*George**	*Nora**	*Dora**	*James*
Prince Roy	*Beulah**	*Ruth**	*Nannie**	*Blanche**

George Monk was born to Rufus and Dollie Monk. He served his country in the U.S. Military for several years. One night, hanging out with several friends, George was involved in a fatal car accident with a train. He is buried over in Murrill Hill Cemetery.

Wright Monk
(September 2, 1894-August 18, 1966)

Wright Monk was the fourth son and fifth child of Daniel and Emma Monk. He was married to Annie Pollock for over 50 years and to this union 13 children were born: Roscoe, Bessie, Matthew, James, Thomas, Haywood, Hedrick, Roxie, Lendsay, Gilbert Leo, George, Vernon and Geneva. His wife Annie; preceded him in death in December 1965 and he passed away the following year, August 1966.

Wright's Family Tree

Wright and Annie Monk

Roscoe*	Bessie*	Matthew*	James*	Thomas*	Haywood*
Patrisia	Elmar			Daisy	Wilber
	Elnora				Rufus*
	David				Rosa
	Bessie*				Johnny
	Katie*				Jimmy
	Ronny				Annie Pearl*
					Sarah
					Haywood, Jr.
					Clementine
					Dexter

*Hedrick**	*Roxie**	*Lendsay**	*Gilbert Leo**
Michael*	Rosa*	Joyce	Evangeline
Timmy*	John L	Lindsey	Gilbert Jr.
Fredericka		Luvenia	Anna Marie
Clanzell		Melody	
		Ernestine	
		Roslyn	

George (Lil Bit)	*Vernon**	*Geneva*
Faye Tina	Annie	Sharon*
Judy Carol	Lovernon	Corinthia
Ray	Christine	Mauricia
Ralph	Cornell	Bernita
Delmar	Priscilla	Geneva
Andre	Maurice	

"Annie Monk with her
daughter Bessie."

Roscoe Monk

Roscoe Monk was the 1st child born to Wright and Annie Monk. He had one daughter, Patricia Monk Underdue.

Bessie Mae Monk Williams (January 23, 1917-August 31, 2002)

Bessie Mae Monk Williams was born on January 23, 1917 to Wright and Anne Pollock Monk. She met and married the late Charlie Williams and to that union six children were born: Elmar, Elnora, David, Bessie,

Katie and Ronny. Today, Bessie's tree includes a host of grandchildren and great grandchildren.

Bessie's Tree

Elmar (Williams) Cancer resides in Rapids Michigan along with her husband Joe Cancer. She has six children. Angeline, Theresa Ann, Unthina, George, Mona Lisa, Edwina. Angeline has 3 girls and 8 boys totaling 11 children and 20 grandchildren. Theresa Ann has two boys and 3 grandchildren. Unthina has 2 boys and 2 girls totaling 4 children and 6 grandchildren. George has two girls and 4 grandchildren. Mona Lisa has 3 girls and two grandchildren. Edwina has 2 boys and 1 girl with a total of 3 grandchildren.

Elnora (Williams) Watkins still lives in Jacksonville, North Carolina. During her younger years she worked for the Onslow County School System for 35 years. Currently she drives a school bus and is listed today as the oldest bus driver in Onslow County. She has one son Dennis "McRoy" Williams and one grandson.

David Mack Williams is the oldest son of Bessie and Charlie Williams. In 1972, David established Williams' Garage and is currently still in business today. David is married to Calamity J. Parker and they have three daughters. Tonka, Treva, Tova and one granddaughter, Thailesha.

Bessie Veronica Williams (Hagler) best known as Babysister, worked in the Onslow County School System for 28 years until cancer took her away. She had one son Grant Chester Hagler, Jr. who is currently living in Atlanta, Georgia. Grant has two daughters and two sons; Veronica, De`Andre, Markiah and a step-son, Juan Miles who has a daughter; Kailah. Veronica will soon add another grandchild to Grant's family tree.

Katie Mae (Williams) Williams, the youngest daughter of Charlie and Bessie Williams passed away December 3, 2006 at the home. Katie graduated from Jacksonville Senior High School. She worked in the Onslow County Schools as a Teacher Assistant for Thirty-three years and drove the school bus for thirty-nine. Katie was married to Charles R. Williams on June 28, 1985. Katie has three children, two daughters; Valerie, Leslie and one son; Charlie D. Williams. Currently, Valerie still resides in Jacksonville, NC where she is currently employed by Onslow

County School System. Leslie lives in Charlotte, NC and works in the Charlotte Mecklenburg School System. Leslie has one son, Bryan D. Williams and one grandson Bryon Williams whom also lives in Charlotte. Charlie D. Williams lives in Concord, North Carolina with his wife Angela and their children, Simone, Charlie II and Michael. Katie has one step daughter LaTasha (Williams) Shaw whom resides in Greenville, North Carolina.

Ronny Steve Edward Williams is the youngest son of Charlie and Bessie Williams. Ronny resides in Jacksonville, North Carolina with his wife Johnnie Mae Kittles Williams. They have three sons Ronny "Fuzz" Williams, Chris Williams and Keith "Turk" Williams. Ronny establish his own business in 1973 Ronny's Muffler Shop on Bell Fork Road, in Jacksonville, NC. Ronny also enjoys Drag-Racing and has won many titles over a 40 year span. Presently, Ronny still drag-races but mostly watches from the side lines and root for his son and friends. Besides drag racing he also farms for a hobby. Ronny "Fuzz" has one son, Tyler. Chris has 5 children, Sa`nyah, Terence, Yontina, Yontre, Yamorie

Ronny and son Keith

Matthew Monk was the third child of Wright and Annie Monk. He died at an early age.

James Monk was the fourth child of Wright and Annie Monk. He also died at an early age.

Thomas Monk was the fifth child of Wright and Annie Monk. He adopted Daisy Burney Porter as his own child.

Haywood Wright Monk (January 29, 1925-August 28, 2003)

Haywood Wright Monk was born on January 29, 1925 to Wright and Annie Monk. He was married to Sara Viola Simmons, they had ten children: Wilber, Rufus, Rosa, Johnny, Jimmy, Annie Pearl, Sarah, Haywood Jr., Clementine, and Dexter. Haywood passed away on August 28, 2003.

Haywood's Family Tree

Sarah "Coakie"

Cathedria—Rico, Tamea
Lisa—Kasyiah, Alani, Roderick
Shakeria
Vanessa
Celine

Clementine "Little Girl"

Christina—"JT", Trinity
Samantha—Sequia, Malik, Tajzah
Allen
Malcolm

Rosie

Andria—Terrell
Shana—Genevieve, Quan

Wilbert

Rufus—Jeffery, Aaliyah, Alona
Terrence—Terrence Jr. "TJ"
Patricia—Cyan

Johnny

Shacora

Shyee
Dayshawn
Trey
Kiaonna—Donte

Dexter

Dexter Jr. "DJ"

Crystal

Annie Pearl *

Theresa Ann—Erica, Antonio
Robert—Robert, Raven
Angela
Clifford—Jamarquis, Olivia
Deanna
Kathy—Sherhonda, Antoniyo, Keondra, Tyniz

Jimmy

Catherina

Carl
Kason
Jessica
Mary

Haywood Jr.

Wanda

Haywood "Little"
Carla
Patricia
Tiffany

Hedrick Randolph Monk (April 28, 1927-March 12, 2004)

Hedrick Randolph Monk was born on April 28, 1927 to Wright and Annie Monk. He was the father of four children: Michael Monk (deceased), Timmy Monk (deceased), Fredericka Monk and Clanzell Monk Brooklyn. Hedrick passed away on March 12, 2004.

Roxie Monk

Roxie Monk Williams was the eighth child of Wright and Annie Monk. She was the mother of two children: Rosa Monk McIntyre and John L. Monk.

Rosa Monk McIntyre was the oldest child of Roxie Monk Williams. She was married to Milton McIntyre. She was the mother of three daughters: Sirrethea Pitts, Winderlee "Windy" Pointe, Versonner "Sonya" McIntyre.

Rosa's Tree

Sirrethea	*Winderlee*	*Versonner*
Dewand—Nakiya, Meshala	Ronetta—Isaiah, Miracle	
LaSwanna—		

Sirrethea currently lives in Charlotte, North Carolina Windy currently lives in Jacksonville, North Carolina; Versonner (Sonya) currently resides in Charlotte, North Carolina, where she is an entrepreneur, creator of

VMack Products (natural cosmetics line) and is also founder of Until Then Ministry (a ministry for disabled homeless women).

John L. Monk was the youngest son of Roxie Monk Williams. He is currently married to Sonya Monk and is both a father, grandfather, great grandfather and Step-father. He currently lives in Jacksonville, North Carolina.

John L Monk's Tree

Bernice Pollock
Shauneice Jones
(Aurnesha Monk;
Santonio Jones; Armani
Reid)
Yontanya Hardison
(Yontina, Yontre,
Yamorie Hardison)
Tamarius Hardison "TQ"
Ra-Kim Hardison
"ROCK"
Co-Shey Pollock

Morena Monk:
Zakia Aubrey
Keimonte Wright

John L. Schaeffer *
Quceria Schaeffer

Tremayne Anchrum:
Shabree Books
Tarryn Anchrum
Tremayne Anchrum,
Jr.
Geo Lopez

Chanell Barksdale:
Erin Barksdale
Lauren Taylor
Terrell Barksdale

Wanda Redding:
Kathryn Redding
Joshua Redding

Karen Williams:

Tracey Mattocks:
Julian Taylor
Jevonte Taylor
Joshua Taylor
Jalen Taylor
Jordan Taylor *

Latoya Mattocks:
Edward Mattocks III
ERIANNA Mattocks
Elijah Mattocks *

Ebony Obewu:
Josiah Lofton
Ninah Obewu
Julia Obewu

Cororomo Dante Bragg:
Elijah Bragg

Eddie Lofton, Jr.:
Leyla Lofton

Lendsay Monk

Lendsay Monk was born on April 8, 1929 to Wright and Annie Monk. At an early age, he went to San Mill to work in order to help his parents out with the younger siblings. In 1960 he took a job as a chief baker at New River Shopping Center where he worked for thirty-three years without ever missing a day. He met and married Mary Hucks in 1954 and to that union six children were born: Joyce, Lindsey (Leon), Luvenia, Melody, Ernestine, and Roslyn. Lendsay was a prolific baker and used his skills for many years. Lendsay passed away on September 9, 2002, only days after his sister Bessie, died.

Lendsay's Tree

Brenda "Joyce"
Kelvin—Raquel, Kelvin Jr.
Herman Jr.,—Alexis
Bridgette—Marissa, Brittany

Arletha "Luvenia"
Grethel

Ernestine
Quinitta Chaunte'
Joshua

Lindsey "Leon"
Step-Daughter Monica—Kendrick,
Monisha, Lineyah

Melody Wooten
Jerpoloyn—Celexia & Lindsey
Jercheaus—
Melody J—Damarius & Dominick

Roslyn Majors
Titus D Majors

Lendsay and Mary are dress as Cat-woman and Batman

Gilbert Leo Monk was the son of Wright and Annie Monk. Gilbert was the father of three children: Evangeline, Gilbert Jr., and Anna Marie.

"Leo" and his wife

George "Lil Bit" Monk

George "Lil Bit" Monk was the eleventh child of Wright and Annie Monk. He is the father of six children: Faye, Judy, Ray, Ralph, Delmar, and Andre. George is currently one of the original living descendants of Daniel and Emma Monk and he lives in Jacksonville, North Carolina.

Vernon Monk

Vernon Monk was born on October 12, 1936 to Wright and Annie Monk. He was the 12th of the 13 children born to Wright and Annie. He met and married Melissa Fonville on November 18, 1962 and they are the parents of six children: Annie, Lovernon, Christine, Cornell, Priscilla, and Maurice. Vernon worked on the Marine Corps Exchange for over 26 years until his retirement. He also worked at several other places throughout Onslow County such as Dutchess Restaurant, Howard Johnson Inn, Chateau Madrid and others. Vernon enjoyed baseball and fishing any chance he could. Sadly, Vernon passed away on Saturday, January 23, 2010 in Jacksonville, North Carolina.

Vernon's Tree

Annie Monk Bush is married to Reginald Bush and they live in Melbourne, Florida.

Lovernon Monk Johnson is married to Robert Johnson and lives in Philadelphia, PA.

Christine Monk Wallace is married to Eric Wallace and they live in Philadelphia, PA and are the parents of Latoya, Lamanda, Aaron, Alyssa, Bryan, and DeShawn.

Lamanda (Monk) Tooley is married to Brian Tooley, and has two children, Elijah and Xavier Tooley. The Tooley's live in Virginia Beach.

Latoya (Monk) Burley is married to Johnniethon Burley, and they have three kids. Their names are Janae, Jaeden, Jylal, and their family lives in Philadelphia.

Cornell Monk resides in Jacksonville, NC.

Priscilla Monk Champion is married to Charlie Champion and they live in Virginia Beach, Virginia.

Maurice Monk is married to Robin Monk and they live in Greensboro, NC.

Geneva Monk Pickett

Geneva Monk Pickett is the youngest child of Wright and Annie Monk. She is also the youngest living grandchild of Daniel and Emma Monk today. She lives in Jacksonville with her husband, Eldon Pickett. She is retired from Onslow County Schools and is an active member of Deliverance Evangelistic Temple. She is also a licensed beautician and loves to cook big family dinners. She is the mother of five daughters: Sharon, Corinthia, Mauricia, Bernita and Geneva Lee and grandmother of 8.

Geneva's Tree

Sharon Pickett was the oldest child of Geneva and Eldon Pickett. She died at an early age.

Corinthia Pickett Lopes is the daughter of Geneva and Eldon Pickett. She is currently a high school math educator at Northside High School in Jacksonville. She is married to Frank Lopes and is the mother of three children: Tiara, Christian, and Daniel.

Mauricia Pickett Jones is the daughter of Geneva and Eldon Pickett. She currently lives in Virginia with her husband, Brian and two children: Brian Jr. and Brittany.

Bernita Fraser is the daughter of Geneva and Eldon Pickett. She currently works aboard Camp Lejeune and lives in Jacksonville. She is also currently engaged to be married and she is the mother of one daughter, Daviana.

Geneva Lee Pickett Golden is the youngest daughter of Geneva and Eldon Pickett. She currently lives in Jacksonville with her husband Kenny Paige-Golden and their two sons: Monte and Kai.

Walter Monk
(March 11, 1897-May 6, 1983)

Walter Monk was the fifth son and sixth child of Daniel and Emma Monk. He married Mary Vann on October 20, 1940 and to this union one daughter was born, Ruth. Walter also took in his younger brother Clarence's daughter, Alneta after he died. He packed his family up and moved down to Wilmington, North Carolina where he is buried in the National Veterans Cemetery.

Walter's Family Tree
Walter and Mary Monk

Ruth (Monk) Jones

Clarence Monk

Clarence Monk was the seventh child and youngest son of Daniel and Emma Monk. He married Mary Hemby and unto this union 7 children were born: Clinny, Marie, Gilbert, Hazel, Helen, Laurel and Alnita. All of Clarence's children are deceased with the exception of Alnita.

Clarence's Family Tree
Clarence and Mary Monk

Clinny*   *Marie**   *Gilbert**   *Hazel**   *Helen**

Laurel*   *Alnita*

Alnita Monk Rollinson   Gilbert Monk

Alnita Monk Rollinson is the youngest child of Clarence and Mary Monk. She was only four years old when her father died and five years old when her mother died. She was subsequently raised by her uncle Walter Monk. She is the only living sibling of Clarence and Mary Monk's children. Alnita is married to Jesse Rollinson and she currently resides in Wilmington, North Carolina.

Lizzie Monk Dixon
(May 1, 1904-August 9, 1979)

Lizzie Monk was the daughter of Daniel and Emma Monk. She met and married Isaac Dixon in October, 1925 and had four children: Roscoe, Inez, Lucenia, and Emma. She was a member of New Dixon Chapel Missionary Baptist Church for a number of years. She passed away on August 9, 1979 and was buried in the Monk Family Cemetery in Murrill Hill.

Lizzie Monk's Family Tree
Lizzie and Isaac Dixon

Roscoe*   *Inez**   *Lucenia*   *Emma**

Lucenia Dixon Hardison is the daughter of Lizzie and Isaac Dixon. She currently lives in Jacksonville, North Carolina and she is a mother and grandchildren.

Other Family Photos and Remembrances

Nancy Monk Murrill and her brother, Ollie "Bud" Monk

Symone Spicer, daughter of LaShanna and Kendall Spicer

Young Monks, descendants of John Moses Monk

Young Monks at Reunion 2008

The Morgan Family during Ricardo's high school graduation, 1997

Young Monks on the Dinner Cruise, Reunion 2008

Mary Monk Dixon and other Monks, 2003

Catherine Monk Morgan, with Daughter-in-law Florene and son Raymond

Rosa McIntyre

Vernon Monk Family

John Daniel Monk's descendants

Geneva with her girls.

Bessie Williams and family
members

Geneva Pickett's daughters   Daphne, Ronald, Sr, Ronald Jr, Ollie Monk
                                                    Henrietta Shepard

The Tooley (Monk) Family

THE DAILY NEWS / DON BRYAN
April 14, 2009

Elnora Watkins stands in front of her number 62 bus at Southwest High School. After 47 years, Elnora has no plans to put brakes on her career as an Onslow County school bus driver.

Watkins is the longest working school bus driver in the county, with a career spanning five decades. Elnora is the daughter of Bessie M. Monk Williams. Check out the local Jacksonville Daily Newspaper for more information on this article.

HOW TO DECORATE A CAKE! Lendsay Monk (L) shows Richlands Piggly Wiggly Deli Manager Donna Bryd just how it's done. Monk, a professional baker and cake decorator has joined the staff at the Deli. With over 42 years experience, Monk worked for Peck's Bakery for 30 years and three other during that period. The Deli now offers, thanks to Monk, fresh bread, do-nuts, cakes, pies, pastries, rolls and subs. "If you want it fresh, we have it," says Bryd. Lendsay has many more newspaper clippings

HOW TO DECORATE A CAKE! Lensay Monk (L) shows Richlands Piggly Wiggly Deli Manager Donna Byrd just how it's done. Monk, a professional baker and cake decorator has joined the staff at the Deli. With over 42 years experience, Monk worked for Peck's Bakery for 30 years and three others during that period. The Deli now offers, thanks to Monk, fresh bread, do-nuts, cakes, pies, pastries, rolls and subs. "If you want it fresh, we have it," says Byrd. (Staff photo - Al Reyer)

Get along, little doggy

Get along, little doggy

Just like a best friend, Bo tagged alongside his owner, Haywood Monk taking a midday stroll down Murrill Hill Road in the Southwest area of Jacksonville to a local store and didn't seem to mind a little canine company.

This is just one of many great articles about Daniel and Emma's Descendants.

Vernon Monk
Sunrise: Sunset:
October 23, 1936 - January 23, 2010
In Loving Memory

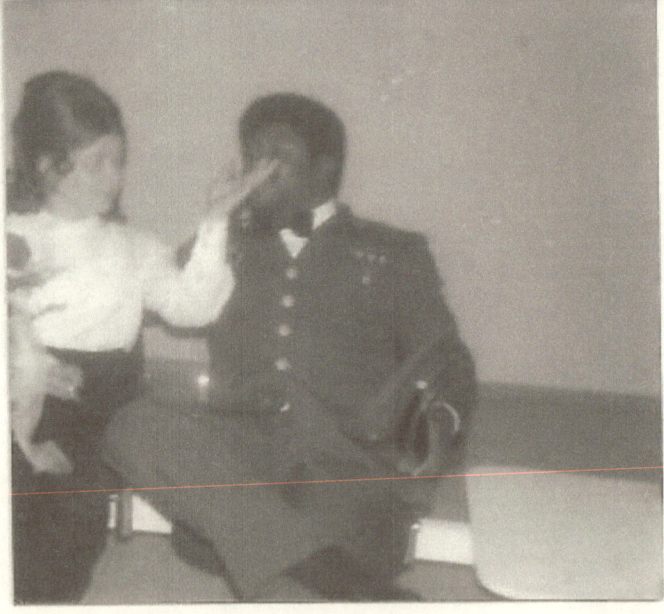

www.ingramcontent.com/pod-product-compliance
Lightning Source LLC
Chambersburg PA
CBHW020358290526
45785CB00005B/2348